Pasbor Chuck,

This is a wonderful little book packed with words, thoughts to ponder. I wanted to share it with you and Pastor Paul. Enjoy!!

God's Peace,

Mary Jo

DIETRICH BONHOEFFER

Wondrously Sheltered

Augsburg Books
MINNEAPOLIS

By Benevolent Powers Wondrously Sheltered

Quietly, loyally surrounded by benevolent
powers,
safeguarded and comforted most wondrously,
these days would I live with you
and with you pass into the new year.

The old year would yet torment our hearts,
the burdens of our dark days yet oppress us,
hence grant, O Lord, to our souls most
distressed
the healing comfort you have prepared for us.

And though the heavy, bitter cup of
suffering you might extend
filled even to the brim,
yet would we accept it without flinching
from your gracious, loving hand.

Shelter

But should you grant us joy once more
in this world and its radiant sun,
then the past let us gratefully recall
and to you entirely our lives devote.

May warmly and brightly glow the candles
you have brought into our darkness today;
if it be possible, bring us together again.
We are sure: your light illuminates our night.

When silence profound now spreads itself around us,
may we yet hear that full voice
of the world unseen around us,
the hymn of praise sung by all your children.

By benevolent powers wondrously sheltered,
we, confident, await what may come.
With us God abides, evening and morn,
more surely still with each dawning day.

$\mathcal{J}$oy draws its nourishment from quietness and from the unfathomable.

Joy

You have a fortunate disposition:

You are able to be happy.

Be happy as much as you can;

joy makes us strong.

To genuinely rejoice means to see God in everything,

As well as his love, there,

wherever things look cheerful and friendly

but also there,

where things are not quite

as you would wish them to be.

That is not so easy.

$\mathcal{T}$oday is a gloomy, rainy day quite suitable to my futile wait
for clarification and enlightenment. But let us not forget for a moment
how much we have to be thankful for and how much goodness we still
experience; I need but think of you, and even the tiniest bit of gloom
in my soul again becomes light.

Excerpted from Dietrich Bonhoeffer's letter to his fiancée, August 12, 1943

Light

In me it is dark, but in you there is light.

I am lonely, but you do not leave me.

I am faint hearted, but with you there is help.

I am restless, but with you there is peace.

In me there is bitterness, but with you there is patience.

I do not understand your ways, but you know

the right way for me.

Where God's word is with me,

I can find my way

even in foreign lands;

I find justice amid injustice,

security amid uncertainty,

strength in work,

and patience in suffering.

Hope

I do not believe that anything that is happening to me is meaningless, and I believe it is better for us all even if it runs contrary to our wishes. In my present existence I actually see a task, one I only hope I will be able to fulfill. From the perspective of the larger goal, any privations and dashed hopes are trivial.

That which is "Christian" rather than being something beyond what is human, instead seeks to be in the midst of what is human. Rather than being an end in itself, it means instead that human beings may and indeed should live as human beings before God.

Faith

We receive only as much faith from God

as we need for the present day.

Faith is the daily bread we receive from God.

With God, one does not just mark time,

rather one walks on a path.

Wishes to which we cling too tightly can easily rob us of some of what we can and indeed ought to be. By contrast, wishes that we repeatedly overcome for the sake of our present tasks make us richer.

The utter lack of wishes is actually poverty. One can have a fulfilled life despite numerous unfulfilled wishes.

Prayer

Prayer is a person's strength.

To pray is to draw breath from God.

To pray means to confide in God.

Prayer is the heart of Christian life.

Your picture hangs before me, the one with which I must now content myself for weeks, but now I again hear your voice. Your laughter — isn't it so, even when we laugh, we are still a bit sad? — I see your eyes, I sense your hand. Everything is wholly real again. How can I thank you for everything? I cannot, I can only tell you that when you are with me, all is well.

Excerpted from Dietrich Bonhoeffer's letter to his fiancée, November 10, 1943

Happiness

This is one of those moments in which one has so much to say that, really, one can only remain silent. One's heart is so full of good, peaceful, grateful thoughts and feels so sheltered from all danger and temptation that it simply would like to offer some of what it itself has so undeservedly received.

Excerpted from Dietrich Bonhoeffer's letter to his fiancée,
Christmas Eve, 1943

$\mathcal{L}$ove can wait a long, long time, till the very end.
It doesn't become impatient, doesn't try to hurry things
or force them to happen.
It expects to wait a good long time.

Love

When two people

know everything about each other,

the mystery of their love becomes

infinitely great between them.

Only within this love do they understand each other,

know all about each other,

fully recognize each other.

And yet, the more they love each other

and know about each other through love,

the more they realize the mystery of their love.

Thus knowledge does not dispel the mystery

but only deepens it.

That the other person is so close to me, that is the greatest mystery.

A person who prays can no longer be afraid,
nor any longer be sad.
Christ is in our prayer, and there God is close to us.

Nearness

Look people in the eye

and you will discover their intentions.

Note how people laugh.

Listen to how they

speak about their parents.

Listen to how they speak about God.

It is not the distant person

who is the greatest mystery,

but rather precisely our neighbor.

Who Am I?

Who am I? They often tell me
that I step out of my cell
calmly and cheerfully and firmly
like a manor lord from his mansion.

Who am I? They often tell me
that I speak freely and cordially and
clearly with my guards,
as if I were the one giving orders.

Who am I? They also tell me
that I am bearing these days of misfortune
with equanimity, smiling and proud,
like someone accustomed to victory.

Darkness

Am I really that which others say I am?
Or am I only that which I know about myself?
Restless, longing, sick, like a bird in a cage,
gasping for breath as if someone were strangling me,
hungry for colors, flowers, for the song of birds,
thirsting for kind words, for human nearness,
trembling in anger at arbitrariness and petty insults,
driven by anticipation of great things,
helplessly worried about friends infinitely removed,
too weary and empty for praying, thinking, creating,
exhausted and ready to say farewell to everything?
Who am I? This one or the other one?
Am I this person today and a different one tomorrow?
Am I both at once? A hypocrite before others
and a despicably pathetic weakling before myself?
Or is what is left within me like a vanquished army
fleeing in disarray before the victory that has already been won?

Who am I? Such lonely questions mock me.
Whoever I am, you know me, and I am yours, O God!

O God,

   great misery has come upon me.

   My cares are about to crush me,

   and I do not know where to turn.

   O God, be compassionate and help me.

   Give me the strength to bear whatever

   you may send,

   do not let fear

   rule over me.

Anxiety and Fear

It is not only anxious fear that is infectious,

but also the calmness and joy

with which we encounter what is laid on us.

Thinking and acting with an eye on the coming generation,

yet being ready, each day, to depart without fear or worry –

that is the disposition that has practically been forced upon us,

and though it is not easy to endure it bravely, it is necessary that we do so.

$\mathcal{F}$ear is a net

which evil casts over us

that we might become ensnared

and fall.

Those who are afraid have

already fallen.

Evil

*O*ne of our most remarkable

and yet irrefutable experiences

is that evil

– often in a surprisingly short span of time –

turns out to be dumb and impractical.

I believe

that God can and indeed intends

to allow good to emerge from evil,

even from the greatest evil.

To that end, he needs people

who make the best

of everything.

I believe

that in every situation of distress

God gives us as much strength to resist

as we need.

But he does not give it to us in advance,

lest we come to rely on ourselves

rather than on him alone.

We must also risk

saying things that may well be open to criticism

if by so doing we are stirring up

questions vital to life itself.

Resistance

*R*esponsibility and freedom are mutually corresponding concepts. Responsibility presupposes freedom substantively – not chronologically – just as freedom can exist only in the exercise of responsibility. Responsibility is human freedom that exists only by being bound to God and neighbor.

Freedom

Daring to do what is right rather than what you may simply want

at the moment, not hovering about in what might be possible,

but courageously seizing what is real,

it is not in the flight of thought but solely in deeds that

one finds freedom.

Leave your anxious hesitation behind and go forth into the storm

of events borne only by God's commandment and by faith,

and freedom will welcome your spirit rejoicing.

*I*t is not from the heavy soil of the earth,
but from the free inclination
and free desire of the spirit,
requiring neither oath nor law,
that a friend is bestowed on a friend.

Friendship

There is hardly a feeling that makes us happier than to sense

that we are able to be something for others.

Nor is it numbers that matter here,

but intensity.

Ultimately the most important thing in life

is precisely our human relationships.

Friendship

$\mathcal{I}$t is only from the peace

between two and three people

that the greater peace

for which we hope

can one day emerge.

Peace

There is no way to peace along the way of safety.

For peace must be dared. It is the great venture.

It can never be made safe.

Peace is the opposite of security.

To demand guarantees is to mistrust,

and this mistrust in turn brings forth war.

To look for guarantees is to want to protect oneself.

Not only do the weak need the strong,
but also the strong cannot exist without the weak.
The elimination of the weak is the death of the community.

Strength

The essence of optimism is not this or that view of the present situation, but strength, the strength to hope where others yield to resignation, the strength to keep one's head high when everything seems to go wrong, the strength to endure setbacks, the strength always to claim the future for oneself instead of yielding it to one's opponent.

Dear Parents, April 14, 1943

Above all else you should know and also really believe that I am doing well.

. . . The kind of violent emotional readjustment prompted by so sudden an arrest, and the fact that one must reorient oneself mentally and come to terms with a completely different situation — all this causes physical considerations to recede entirely and become unimportant; and actually I find that this is a genuine enrichment of my experience. Being alone is, after all, not really something to which I am unaccustomed, as is the case with many people, and it is certainly a good steam bath for the soul. The only thing that torments me is or would be the idea that you are yourselves anxious and tormented because of me, and that you are not sleeping and eating properly.

Consolation

I am alone.

There is no one to whom I might pour out my heart.

So I pour it out to myself

and to the God

to whom I cry out.

It is good

to pour out one's heart

in loneliness

rather than to let care

eat away at us.

*E*ach new morning is a new beginning of our life.
Each day is a concluded whole.

Trust

We know

that one of the most reprehensible things

is to sow and encourage mistrust,

and that wherever possible,

we should instead strengthen and foster trust.

Trust will always remain

one of the greatest,

rarest, and happiest gifts

of human life together.

DIETRICH BONHOEFFER: A Brief Biography

Dietrich Bonhoeffer was born on February 4, 1906, in Breslau, Germany. His father, Karl, was Professor of Neurology and Psychiatry, and his mother, Paula, was a committed Christian, who devoted herself to running the household and raising their eight children.

Dietrich was a sensible, gifted, and clever child. Along with his siblings — Susanne, Sabine, Christine, Ursula, Klaus, Walter, and Karl-Friedrich — he received religious instruction from his mother from the time he was very young. When Dietrich was six years old, the Bonhoeffer family moved to Berlin. There he attended prep school (*Gymnasium*), subsequently studying theology at the University of Berlin and receiving his second doctorate at the age of twenty-four.

In addition to his vocation as a pastor, he next studied in New York and later in Berlin. Important trips to Italy and New York greatly affected his personality and attitude. But in 1933 his life was fundamentally changed when Adolf Hitler seized power. From then on he engaged passionately in the church's opposition to Hitler's regime. Resistance was forbidden by law, but for Bonhoeffer it stood within the context of love for those who had to endure severe injustice.

In October 1933 Bonhoeffer went to London, where he served as a pastor for two years. While he was there, he often reported on the actions of the National Socialists (Nazis) in Germany. Later, on the Danish island of Fanö, he gave many notable speeches on peace. And due to his untiring engagement in further political activities as well as connections with Jews, he drew even more scrutiny from the Nazi regime.

Back again in Germany, he undertook the leadership of the illegal seminary in Finkenwalde near Stettin, which was forcibly closed shortly thereafter by the police. Bonhoeffer pursued his work with the underground, and finally in 1940 he was officially banned from teaching, preaching, or publishing.

Bonhoeffer took a second trip to America in the summer of 1939, but he broke it off after six weeks. While he knew that it had become dangerous for him in Germany, it was impossible for him to leave his family and

friends alone in those difficult times. Up until then, Bonhoeffer's resistance had all been within the context of the church; but after his return it became political.

When he was thirty-seven, Bonhoeffer met the eighteen-year-old Maria von Wedemeyer, to whom he became engaged in January 1943. But they were never married, as Bonhoeffer's conspiratorial work was discovered. The Gestapo arrested him on April 5, 1943. This began his incarceration in Tegel Prison. After an unsuccessful assassination attempt on Adolf Hitler, he was moved to the main Gestapo prison on Prinz-Albert-Strasse (Berlin).

In February 1945, Bonhoeffer was taken to Buchenwald concentration camp and finally to the Flossenbürg concentration camp. It was there, on April 9, 1945 (shortly before the end of World War II), that he was condemned and executed on Hitler's order, together with other resistance fighters.

Bonhoeffer's life and writings bear witness to a person who became engaged without qualification on behalf of humanity, and who did so with courage, intelligence, and confidence. His *Letters and Papers from Prison*, published after the war and including various writings that friends had managed to smuggle out of prison, made Bonhoeffer the most widely read theologian of our time. Among other writings, that volume includes the well-known poems "By Benevolent Powers Wondrously Sheltered" and "Who Am I?" both of which reflect his thoughts and feelings during his imprisonment. Alongside his engagement in both the church and the resistance, Bonhoeffer's theological work also continued to be of significance to him. Those works include his doctoral dissertation, *Sanctorum Communion*, his second dissertation, *Act and Being*, as well as *Discipleship*, *Life Together*, and *Ethics*.

Source Credits:

Pages 8, 16, 17: *Brautbriefe Zelle 92: Dietrich Bonhoeffer-Maria von Wedemeyer 1943-1945*, hrsg. Ruth-Alice von Bismark und Ulrich Kabitz, C. H. Beck, München. Translated by Douglas W. Stott.

All other excerpts from: *Dietrich Bonhoeffer Werke* by Dietrich Bonhoeffer. 17 vols. Edited by Eberhard Bethge et al. Munich and Gütersloh: Chr. Kaiser/Gütersloher Verlagshaus, 1986-99. English translation: *Dietrich Bonhoeffer Works*. 17 vols. Wayne Whitson Floyd Jr., General Editor. Minneapolis: Fortress Press 1996-.

Excerpts from page 36 from DBW 5: *Gemeinsames Leben Das Gebetbuch der Bibel*. Edited by Gerhard Ludwig Müller and Albrecht Schönherr: Chr. Kaiser/Gütersloher Verlagshaus, 1987. English translation: *Life Together and Prayerbook of the Bible*. Edited by Geffrey B. Kelly. Translated by Daniel W. Bloesch and James H. Burtness. Minneapolis: Fortress Press, 2005, page 96.

Excerpts from page 12 from DBW 6: *Ethik*. Edited by Ilse Tödt, Heinz Eduard Tödt, Ernst Feil, and Clifford Green: Chr. Kaiser/Gütersloher Verlagshaus, 1992, page 404. Translated by Douglas W. Stott.

Excerpts from pages 4, 5, 9, 11, 22-25, 27-33, 37, 38, 41, 14 come from DBW 8: *Widerstand und Ergebung*. Edited by Christian Gremmels, Eberhard Bethge, Renate Bethge, and Ilse Tödt. Gütersloh: Chr. Kaiser/Gütersloher Verlagshaus, 1998, pages 607f, 204f, 421, 513f, 208, 36, 226, 29, 30, 202, 283, 571, 586, 567, 36, 43f, 31, 258f. All pages translated by Douglas W. Stott except page 30 translated by Reinhard Krauss.

Excerpts from pages 15, 20, 21, 7 from DBW 10: *Barcelona, Berlin, Amerika 1928-1931*. Edited by Reinhart Staats, Hans Christoph von Hase, Holger Roggelin, and Matthias Wünsche: Chr. Kaiser/Gütersloher Verlagshaus, 1991, pages 544, 573, 544, 540f. Translated by Douglas W. Stott.

Excerpts from page 6 from DBW 12: *Berlin 1932-1933*. Edited by Carsten Nicolaisen and Ernst-Albert Scharffenorth: Chr. Kaiser/Gütersloher Verlagshaus, 1997, page 458. Translated by Douglas W. Stott.

Excerpts from pages 21, 35, 26, 18, 19 from DBW 13: *London 1933-1935*. Edited by Hans Goedeking, Martin Heimbucher, and Hans-Walter Schleicher: Chr. Kaiser/Gütersloher Verlagshaus, 1994, pages 360, 300, 345, 388, 361. All pages translated by Douglas W. Stott except pages 35, 18, 19 translated by Isabel Best.

Excerpts from pages 39, 40 from DBW 14: *Illegale Theologenausbildung Finkenwalde 1935-1937*. Edited by Otto Dudzus, Jürgen Henkys, Sabine Bobert-Stützel, Dirk Schulz, and Ilse Tödt: Chr. Kaiser/Gütersloher Verlagshaus, 1996, pages 854, 871. Translated by Douglas W. Stott.

Excerpts from pages 34, 13b, 10 from DBW 15: *Illegale Theologenausbildung Sammelvikariate 1937-1940*. Edited by Dirk Schulz: Chr. Kaiser/Gütersloher Verlagshaus, 1998, pages 272, 508, 530. All pages translated by Douglas W. Stott except page 13b translated by Claudia Bergmann-Moore.

Excerpt from page 13a source unknown. Translated by Douglas W. Stott.

ISBN: 0-8066-5281-0

First English-language edition published by Augsburg Books in 2006.

Original German edition Copyright © 2006 by Gütersloher Verlagshaus, Gütersloh, Verlagsgruppe Random House GmbH, München.

Cover design: schwecke.mueller Werbeagentur GmbH, München
Cover image: getty images, Munich
Interior photos: Wolfgang Kabisch, Gütersloh
Biography photos: Archives Gütersloher Verlagshaus, Gütersloh
Reproduction: redhead, Steinhagen
Printing and Binding: Těšínská Tiskárna, Český Těšín
Printed in Czech Republic

09 08 07 06 05   1 2 3 4 5 6 7 8 9 10